GOVERNMENT & DEMOCRACY

VOTE!

OUR VALUES

by
Charlie Ogden

THE SECRET BOOK COMPANY

©2020
The Secret Book Company
King's Lynn, Norfolk PE30 4LS

ISBN: 978-1-78998-074-5

Written by:
Charlie Ogden

Edited by:
Grace Jones

Designed by:
Drue Rintoul

CONTENTS

Words that look like **this** can be found in the glossary on page 31.

WHAT IS A GOVERNMENT?

A government is a group of people put in place by a **society**. It provides rules, **authority** and order for the people in that society. Today, most countries in the world have a government.

For many countries this is a good thing, as a government should try to organise the people and **resources** in a country in the way that is best for its **citizens**. However, while governments are supposed to do all they can to help the people in their countries, some governments are more effective at doing this than others.

POLITICS INVOLVES DISCUSSING QUESTIONS AND HAVING DEBATES ABOUT HOW A GOVERNMENT SHOULD BE RUN.

The Grand Kremlin Palace in Moscow, Russia, is home to the president of the Russian government.

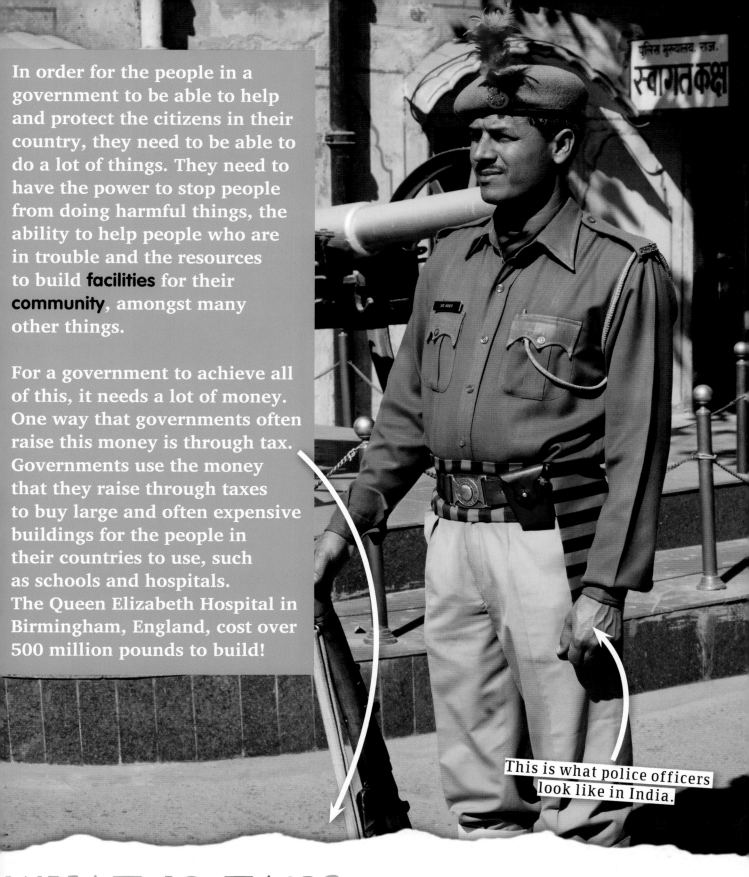

In order for the people in a government to be able to help and protect the citizens in their country, they need to be able to do a lot of things. They need to have the power to stop people from doing harmful things, the ability to help people who are in trouble and the resources to build **facilities** for their **community**, amongst many other things.

For a government to achieve all of this, it needs a lot of money. One way that governments often raise this money is through tax. Governments use the money that they raise through taxes to buy large and often expensive buildings for the people in their countries to use, such as schools and hospitals. The Queen Elizabeth Hospital in Birmingham, England, cost over 500 million pounds to build!

This is what police officers look like in India.

WHAT IS TAX?

Tax is the money that the people pay to their government so that the government can do things such as pay for police officers, help people with health problems and build schools, roads and hospitals.

WHY IS A GOVERNMENT IMPORTANT?

Sometimes people find it difficult to understand why having a government is important. One person who believed that having a government was important was the **philosopher** Thomas Hobbes. He asked people to think about what life would be like without a government. He believed that if there was no government, people would be more likely to commit crimes, such as coming into your home and taking whatever they wanted, because there would be no laws or police officers to stop them. Governments help to provide protection and safety to the people that they govern; they try to make it so that a community of people can live and work together peacefully.

Thomas Hobbes

MONEY

Money is very important for communities all around the world because it allows people to buy things that they need. Without governments, however, it is unlikely that our system of money would work as well as it does. This is because governments are the ones who are able to organise a country's citizens into agreeing that the pieces of paper and metal, which we call money, actually mean something.

If you think about it, money doesn't actually have any value itself; you can't eat it as food or make clothes out of it. Money only has value because everyone agrees that it has value. For example, a butcher knows that the money he makes selling bacon can be used to buy anything else he wants. Without a government, people might not be certain that the money they have could be used to buy other things.

THE OLDEST COIN EVER FOUND WAS DISCOVERED IN TURKEY AND IS OVER 2,700 YEARS OLD.

DISASTERS

Natural disasters, such as floods and earthquakes, may leave people homeless, in a great amount of danger and without food or water. When this happens, governments are some of the only people who can provide **aid** on a large scale, because they have the resources and money to do so. Governments will often have emergency money that is only allowed to be spent in disaster situations.

During floods, for example, governments may send boats to the people who are trapped by the flood waters, use parachutes to drop in food supplies from aeroplanes and work to reduce the level of the flood waters – all at the same time! If the disaster is particularly bad, a government can also organise fund-raising schemes or ask governments in other countries for additional help.

In 2015, the British Army was sent in by the UK government to provide aid during floods in York, England.

LAWS

One of the most important things that a government can do for a country is make its laws. These are rules that everyone in a country must follow. A country's laws are meant to protect the people in that country. People who do not follow the law are committing a crime, which they can be punished for. A person may have to go to prison, pay a fine or work within the community for free as part of their punishment.

However, even though it is the government that decides what should become law, often a country's citizens are able to influence the government's decision. Sometimes the opinions of the public, as well as pressure from the media, can push a government to pass a law. This is because governments know that they should try to listen to public opinion because they have been chosen to represent the people of that country.

Fox hunting was banned in the UK in 2004 due to pressure from the public and the media.

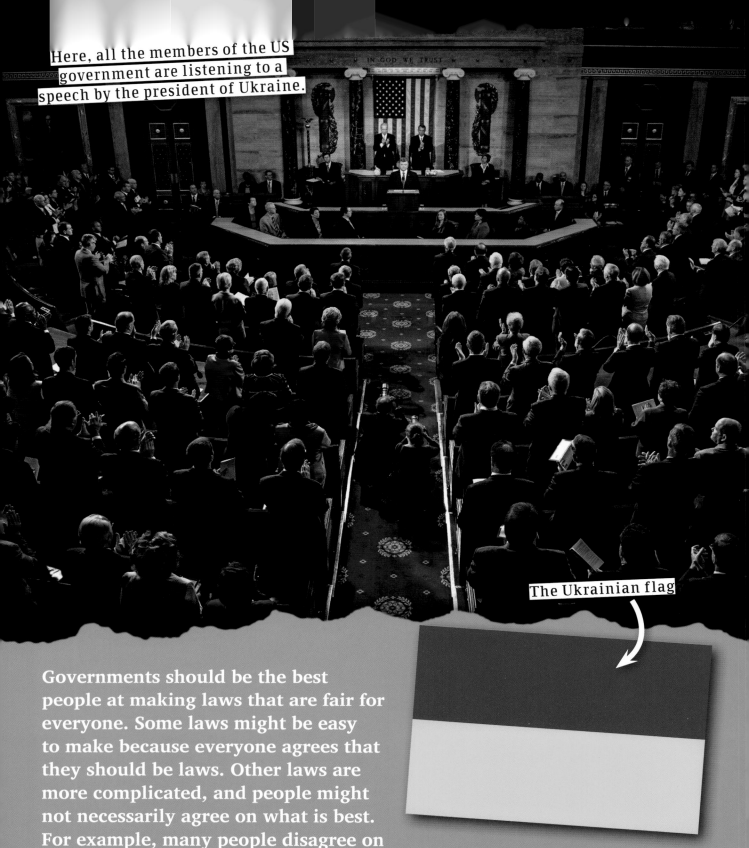

Here, all the members of the US government are listening to a speech by the president of Ukraine.

The Ukrainian flag

Governments should be the best people at making laws that are fair for everyone. Some laws might be easy to make because everyone agrees that they should be laws. Other laws are more complicated, and people might not necessarily agree on what is best. For example, many people disagree on how much tax different people should pay. Governments should be the best at deciding these things because they have the resources that are needed to work out what would be best for everyone.

Governments should also be the best at making laws because they should be made up of lots of different people from all different backgrounds. If just one person made all the laws, they could make laws that only help them.

LAWS AROUND THE WORLD

A government can usually only make laws for its own country. This means that different countries around the world sometimes have very different laws. In the UK, there are laws that state that **equality** must exist between all people. However, not all governments have such laws. In fact, some governments around the world have laws that stop people from being equal.

For example, women weren't allowed to drive in Saudi Arabia until 2017 – before this, only men could. This meant that men and women weren't considered equal in the eyes of the law. Luckily, after campaigning and protesting, the law was changed. Now, women in Saudi Arabia are allowed to drive. However, lots of countries still have laws that stop people from being seen as equal.

PRIME MINISTERS AND PRESIDENTS

Governments are organised in many different ways, some of which are very complicated. However, most governments will have a single person who is considered to be the head of that government. This person is usually called a prime minister or president.

This is Margaret Thatcher. She was prime minister of the UK from 1979 to 1990.

UK GOVERNMENT

In the UK, the head of the government is called the prime minister. The two most important parts of the UK government are the prime minister and the cabinet. The cabinet is made up of 23 senior members of the government, including the prime minister who chooses the other 22 members. Every week, the members of the cabinet and the prime minister come together to discuss the most important issues that the government is facing at that particular time. It is the job of the UK government to develop new **policies**, make sure that all policies are being followed and to put forward suggestions for new laws.

PARLIAMENT

Even though it is the government that suggests new laws in the UK, it cannot **officially** make a new law until Parliament has agreed to it. Parliament is a group of over 1,000 people who are responsible for debating the suggestions of the government and approving, amending or voting against new laws that the government may want to create. This means that Parliament doesn't suggest new ways to run the country. Instead, it can only accept, amend or reject the ideas put forward by the government.

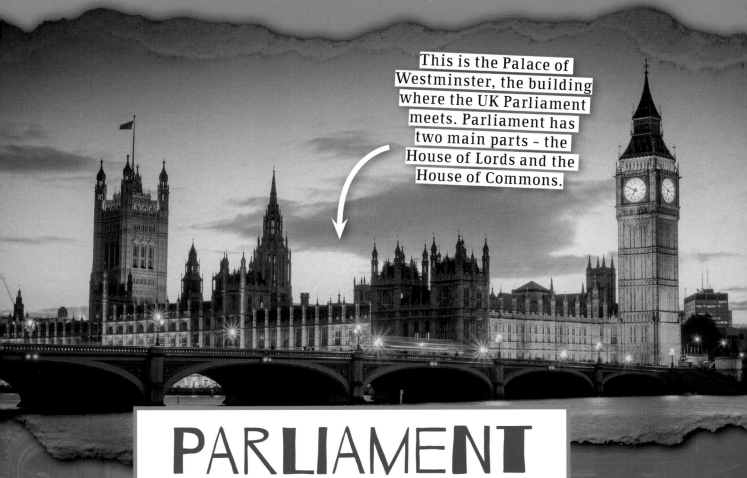

This is the Palace of Westminster, the building where the UK Parliament meets. Parliament has two main parts – the House of Lords and the House of Commons.

PARLIAMENT

HOUSE OF LORDS

Made up of people chosen by the prime minister or an independent organisation. There are also **hereditary** members. There are around 800 members of the House of Lords and the number keeps rising every year!

HOUSE OF COMMONS

Made up of Members of Parliament (MPs) who have been **elected** by the public. There are 650 members of the House of Commons.

US GOVERNMENT

In the US, the head of the government is called the president. However, the president is only one part of the US government. When the United States of America first became a country, a document was written that explained how the government should be set up and how the country should be run. This document is called the Constitution of the United States and it explains that the US government should have three parts so that no individual person or group can ever have too much power.

Barack Obama, the 44th President of the US

US GOVERNMENT

CONGRESS	THE PRESIDENT	THE SUPREME COURT
NUMBER OF PEOPLE:	NUMBER OF PEOPLE:	NUMBER OF PEOPLE:
535	1	9

CONGRESS

The role of Congress in the US government is very similar to that of the House of Commons in the UK government. They are a group of people who are responsible for suggesting, amending and deciding new laws and policies for the country.

THE PRESIDENT

The president is the most important person in the US government. The president has to agree that the new laws and policies suggested by Congress are going to benefit the American people. It is the president's job to work out the most effective way to put them into action.

THE SUPREME COURT

The job of the Supreme Court is to make sure that none of the new laws suggested by Congress go against what is said in the US Constitution. The Supreme Court also decides what certain laws actually mean in cases where it is uncertain whether a law has been broken or not.

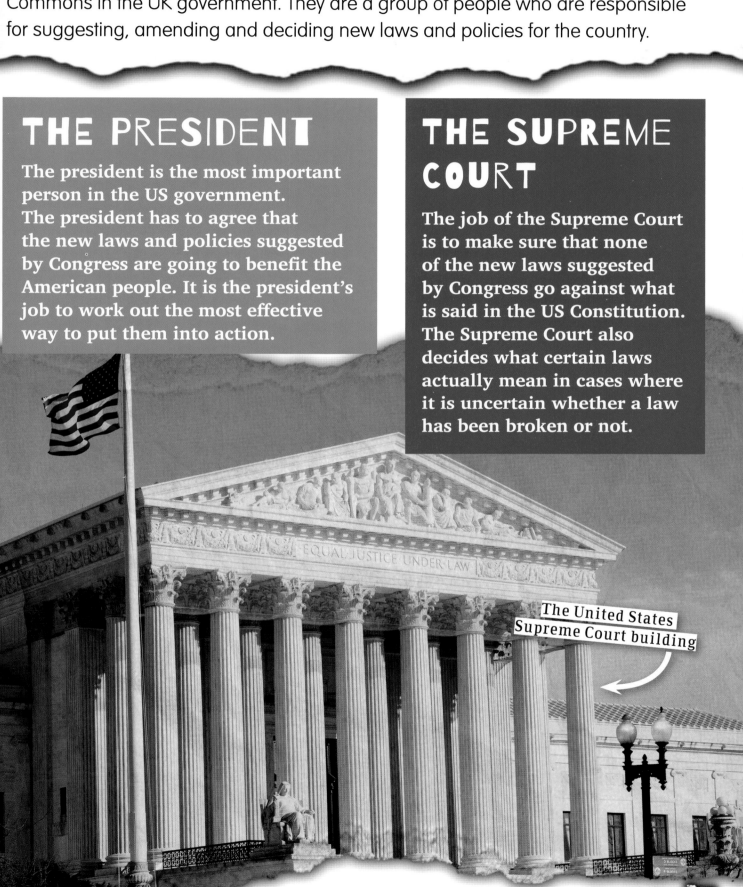

The United States Supreme Court building

GOVERNMENTS AROUND THE WORLD

JAPAN

The Japanese flag

Japan formed a new government in 1947, after **World War Two**, and wrote a **constitution** that explained how the new government should run the country. There is a specific part of the Japanese Constitution that is unlike the constitution of any other government in the world – it **prohibits** Japan from ever going to war. Japan has not fought a war against another country since World War Two and if it follows its own constitution, it never will. Japan still has an army, but it cannot use it to attack other countries. Instead, the army has remained in case Japan is attacked by another country and needs to defend itself.

Japan

Tokyo, the capital city of Japan

NORTH KOREA

The government of North Korea is one of the most well-known governments in the world. North Korea became a country in 1948 and when it did, a man called Kim Il-sung was made the president. Since then, many people believe that the North Korean government has become a dictatorship, as rule over the country has passed from father to son without a **democratic** election.

DICTATORSHIP

A dictatorship is a form of government where one person, or sometimes a small group of people, makes all of the decisions for a country. (For more information, see page 23.)

Pyongyang, the capital city of North Korea

North Korea

The North Korean flag

The North Korean government has been run this way for over 60 years. Because of this, decisions have been made that seem to benefit the government rather than the public. The North Korean dictator, Kim Jong-un, and many people who are close to him, seem to live expensive lifestyles in big houses, whereas much of the North Korean population don't appear to have enough money to live comfortably. However, it is difficult to be exactly sure what is going on in North Korea. It is one of the most secretive countries in the world and the government lets very few people enter the country.

BHUTAN

Bhutan is a very small country in Asia. In 1972, Bhutan introduced a policy that would change the way that **politicians** around the world thought about the success of governments. The king of Bhutan, known as Dragon King Jigme Singye Wangchuck, declared that the happiness of the people in Bhutan should be used to measure how well the country's government was doing. In Bhutan, Gross National Happiness is the most important factor in measuring the government's success or failure.

The Bhutanese flag

This is the United Nations (UN) flag. The UN is an important organisation that works with governments all over the world. They have, along with Bhutan, made happiness one of their main considerations when deciding how successful a government is.

Bhutan

Thimphu, the capital city of Bhutan

SOMALIA

Somalia was once a very powerful country. However, in recent years it has had one of the most unstable governments in the world. In 1991, a **civil war** broke out in Somalia and the Somali government was removed from power by some of the Somali public. A new government could not be formed in Somalia for many years as the civil war and a severe **drought** used much of the country's resources. This made it very difficult for people to make positive changes in Somalia and the country was left in a state of **anarchy**.

In 2000, a Somali government was established for the first time in nearly ten years. However, this new government was only ever in control of a very small amount of Somalia, leaving most of Somalia's population to survive the civil war without help from a government.

The Somali flag

Mogadishu, the capital city of Somalia

Somalia

The Somali parliament finally met in 2012, after over a dozen attempts to create a new government. By this time, most of the country had spent over 20 years living without a government.

WHAT IS A DEMOCRACY?

Living within a democracy means that people get to take part in the decisions made by their government – they are able to have a say in how their country is governed. Any kind of government that is influenced by public opinion is called a democracy; however, this doesn't mean that all democracies are the same. In the past, it used to be the case that only men, or even just rich men, could take part in the decisions of a government. Today, lots of countries accept that everyone should have a say in a democracy and usually the only condition is that you have to be above a certain age.

There are two main types of democracy; a direct democracy and a representative democracy. These two types of democracy relate to the ways in which people can take part in the decisions of their governments.

DIRECT AND REPRESENTATIVE DEMOCRACIES

A direct democracy is where the public can vote on every decision made by their government. This is often not a realistic way to run a government, especially in countries with lots of people. Governments in big countries have to make lots of decisions and there often isn't enough time to find out what everyone in the country wants the government to do.

People in representative democracies instead vote on who is in their government. Every few years, people in representative democracies can vote on who they want to govern their countries – these are called **general elections**. After the votes have been counted and a government has been chosen, the people in that country usually do not get to vote on individual laws or policies. Instead, they trust that the government they voted for will make the right decisions. If the public feel that the government is not representing their interests, they can choose to vote for a different party or politician in the next general election.

The UK government is a representative democracy and usually has a general election every five years. The two biggest **political parties** in the UK are Conservative and Labour.

VOTE FOR CHANGE

Vote Conservative

VOTE Labour

Labour

vote labour

labour.org.uk

Labour

WHAT ISN'T A DEMOCRACY?

MONARCHY

Another way of governing a country is through a monarchy. This is where one member of a royal family, called the monarch, rules over a country. While every member of the ruling family in a monarchy will have some power, only the monarch is considered to be the leader of the country. When the monarch dies, another member of the same family takes over, usually their eldest son. In Europe, a person who rules a monarchy is usually called a king or a queen, whereas in Asia they are often called an emperor or an empress.

Queen Elizabeth II is technically the ruler of the UK, but the democratic government makes almost all of the important decisions.

There are very few monarchies left in the world today and many that do still exist don't really count as monarchies. This is because the kings, queens, emperors or empresses in these countries do not have much actual power. Instead, these countries often have a democratic government that runs the country and looks after its people.

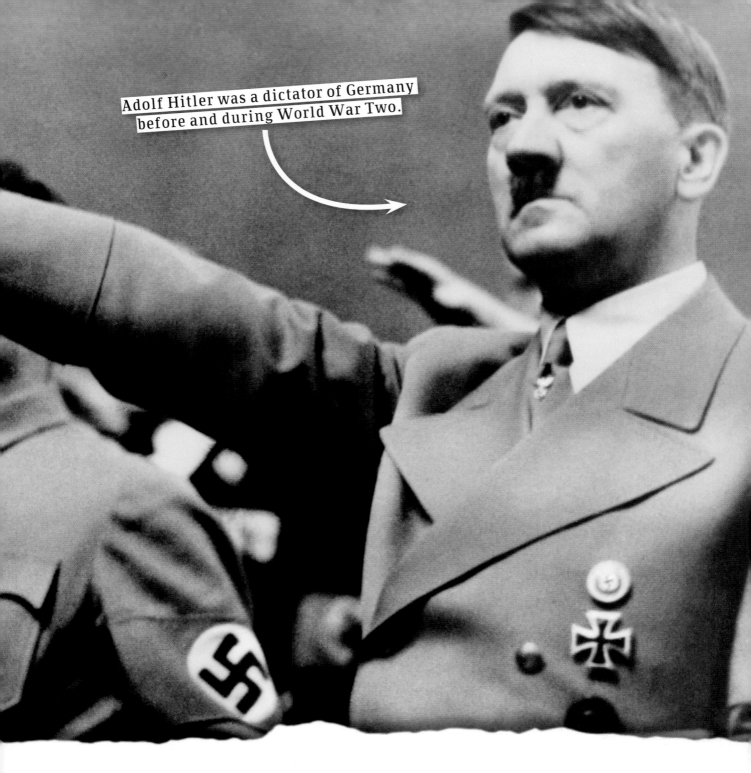

Adolf Hitler was a dictator of Germany before and during World War Two.

DICTATORSHIP

The leader of a dictatorship, known as a dictator, can gain power in a number of ways. Sometimes they work their way up through a democratic government and then, when they have enough power to do so, they change the government into a dictatorship and put themselves in charge. Other times, civil war may break out in the country. During a civil war, a group of people who want there to be a change in their country's government might force the government out of power and put their own dictator in charge instead.

WHY IS A DEMOCRACY IMPORTANT?

Democratic governments have been shown to produce two outcomes in particular: the freedom of their people and a **stable government**. Democracy is important because it often leads to these two things.

In 2017, after many protests, marches and discussions, Australia legalised same-sex marriage. This shows how democracy can be used to provide a country with freedom and equal rights.

Most people want the freedom to choose what religion they follow, where they live and who they marry. Most democracies encourage freedom as they listen to, and act upon, the views and beliefs of the people they govern. For something to become law in a democratic government, a majority of people have to agree that it should be a law. Often, extreme views about marriage, religion and where people should live aren't held by a majority of people. This stops extreme views from being made into laws in democratic governments, meaning that citizens in democratic countries often have their freedom.

Democratic countries, if run properly, often have the support of most of their citizens. This is because they are run by publicly elected politicians who usually try to represent the public's interests. This greatly reduces the chance of civil war in democratic countries as people are not likely to attack a government that they agree with.

Countries that are run by a dictator, on the other hand, are more likely to break out into civil war. Dictators can do anything they want with their countries and are almost always unelected. This can lead to some people starting a civil war in order to remove the dictator.

In 2011, a civil war broke out in Libya in order to overthrow the dictator Muammar Gaddafi.

DEMOCRACY IN HISTORY

Many people believe that the principles of democracy were first founded over 2,500 years ago in the ancient city of Athens. Athens is now the capital city of Greece. However, at that point in time, it was an independent city that acted much like a country does today.

This is the Parthenon, a temple dedicated to the ancient Greek goddess Athena. It was built when Athens was first a democracy, roughly 2,500 years ago.

Until this point in history, nearly all countries were controlled by a monarch or a dictator. Because of this, a lot of people in Athens at the time were interested and excited by the idea of democracy. However, there was one person in particular who did not like the idea of Athens being a democracy – Plato. Plato was a famous philosopher who lived thousands of years ago in Athens. He thought that democracy was a bad idea because most people are not capable of running a country. He believed that the people of Athens would only make poor decisions about how to run the city and that a better idea would be to let only the most intelligent people in Athens have a say in how the city was run.

Athens had a direct democracy, meaning that the public could vote on every decision made by the government. However, in many ways, the democracy in Athens wasn't a very good democracy.

The main way in which the government in Athens failed to be a good democracy was that it didn't allow everyone to vote. Only men over the age of 18 could vote – slaves, women and children had no say in what the government did.

However, this was not very unusual for the time. In the UK, women were not given the same right to vote as men until 1928. Even though the democratic government in ancient Athens wasn't perfect, it was still very ahead of its time.

The Acropolis of Athens

Athens was conquered around 2,400 years ago and became a monarchy under the rule of King Philip II of Macedonia. Athens had a democratic government for fewer than 200 years and only returned to a democratic system some 2,000 years later.

DEMOCRACY AROUND THE WORLD

Sometimes it can be very difficult to know whether a country has a democratic government or not. This is because governments are often very large and have a lot of different parts to them. This can sometimes mean that one part of a government works democratically and another part doesn't work democratically.

Lots of studies have been done in order to determine which countries are democratic and which are not. Some countries in Africa and Asia do not have democratic governments, but instead are ruled by some sort of dictatorship. Other countries in Africa and Asia, and some in South America, have governments that have some elements of a democracy and some elements of a dictatorship. This is a good sign – it shows that countries in these areas are beginning to move towards a democratic form of government.

Most democratic governments today exist in western Europe, North America and South America. However, there are strong democratic governments outside of these areas, such as in Australia, Japan, South Africa and India. India is the largest democratic country in the world – over 800 million people were able to vote in the last general election.

The most democratic countries in the world, according to the Democracy Index, are in northern Europe. Norway, Sweden, Denmark and other countries in the same area of Europe are believed by many to have the most stable and democratic governments in the world.

This is possibly because of the size of these countries. Many of the countries in this area of Europe are very small and have populations of fewer than 10 million people. This makes it a lot easier to maintain a strong democratic government and collect votes from everyone in the country. However, this can't be the only reason that they are democratic, as there are lots of countries that are even smaller than these that do not have democratic governments.

A man in India's capital city, New Delhi

ACTIVITIES

1 Be like Thomas Hobbes! In what ways would life change if there were no governments giving rules, order and protection to communities?

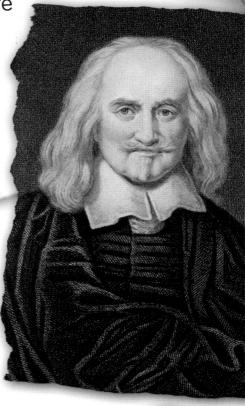

2 Look at the map below and pick a country. Now use the internet to find out what type of government it has.

GLOSSARY

aid — help given to people in a disaster by a government or charity

anarchy — a complete lack of government or law within a country, which can lead to confusion and wild behavior

authority — the power to give orders or make decisions

citizens — legally recognised members of a country

civil war — a war between citizens of the same country

community — a group of people who live and work in the same area

constitution — a collection of rules that state how a government should work

democratic — related to or supported by democracy

drought — a long period of very little rainfall, which leads to a lack of water

elected — voted for by the public

equality — the state of being equal, especially in rights, status and opportunity

facilities — buildings or pieces of equipment provided for a specific purpose

general elections — where the main parties in governments are voted for by the public

hereditary — passed down from a parent to a child

officially — with the authority of the government

philosopher — a person who studies the nature of knowledge, reality and existence

policies — courses of action adopted by organisations or governments

political parties — organised groups of people who have similar ideas about government

politicians — people who are professionally involved in the government and politics

prohibits — to formally forbid someone from doing something according to the law or rules

resources — supplies of money, materials or people

society — a large collection of people made up of many communities

stable government — a government that is resistant to sudden change or collapse

World War Two — a major war fought between 1939 and 1945

INDEX